For the Mountain Laurel Waldorf School –
you will always be home ~ G.S.

For my mum ~ M.G.

First published 2020 by Walker Books Ltd, 87 Vauxhall Walk, London SE11 5HJ • This edition published 2022
Storyline © 2020 Gideon Sterer • Illustrations © 2020 Mariachiara Di Giorgio • The right of Gideon Sterer
and Mariachiara Di Giorgio to be identified as author and illustrator respectively of this work has been
asserted by them in accordance with the Copyright, Designs and Patents Act 1988 • This book has been typeset
in Futura T • Printed in China All rights reserved. No part of this book may be reproduced, transmitted or
stored in an information retrieval system in any form or by any means, graphic, electronic or mechanical,
including photocopying, taping and recording, without prior written permission from the publisher. British
Library Cataloguing in Publication Data: a catalogue record for this book is available from the British Library
ISBN 978-1-4063-9465-8 www.walker.co.uk • 10 9 8 7 6 5 4 3 2 1

THE MIDNIGHT FAIR

Gideon Sterer   illustrated by Mariachiara Di Giorgio

WALKER BOOKS
AND SUBSIDIARIES
LONDON · BOSTON · SYDNEY · AUCKLAND

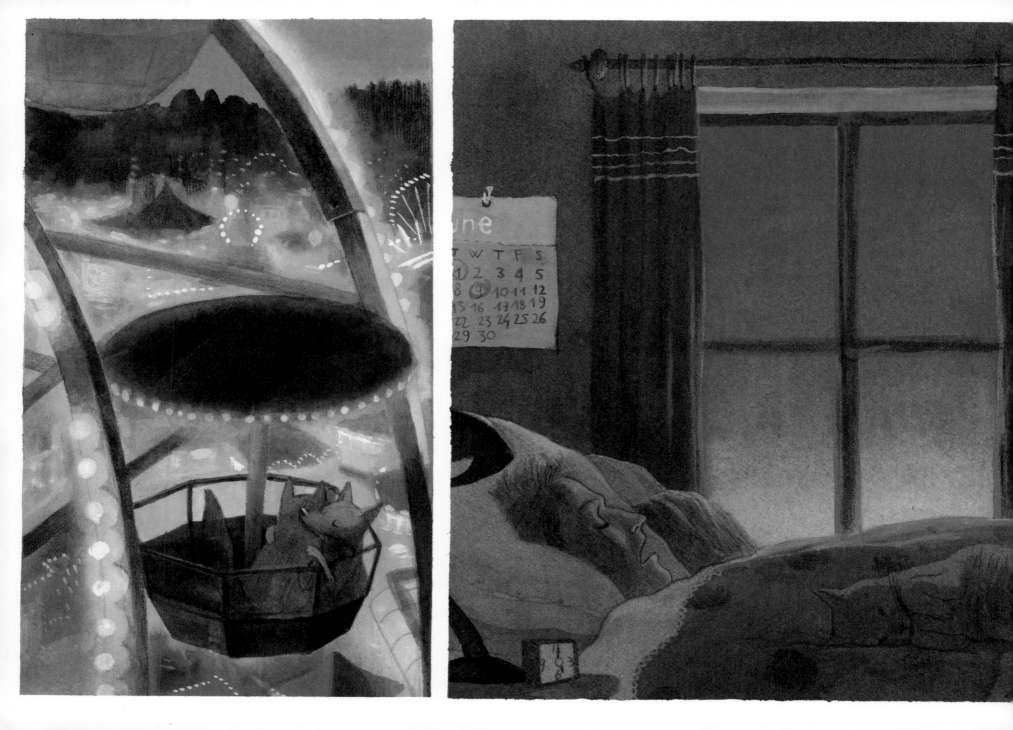

"Surreal and striking, Di Giorgio's artwork is full of magic and wonder" *The Scotsman*

"Gorgeously whimsical and utterly convincing" *Kirkus Reviews (Starred Review)*

"Di Giorgio creates the sense that viewers are part of the crowd, and bathes every spread in brilliant, theatrical light" *Publishers Weekly (Starred Review)*

"Children will savour this glorious, wordless night to remember" *Booklist (Starred Review)*

"Wordless and eloquent" *The Wall Street Journal*

Gideon Sterer is an award-winning American author whose books include *Not Your Nest!*, illustrated by Andrea Tsurumi, *From Ed's to Ned's*, illustrated by Lucy Ruth Cummins and *The Christmas Owl*, co-written with Ellen Kalish and illustrated by Ramona Kaulitzki. Gideon grew up in the woods of upstate New York, where his parents owned a little zoo where he would run around after-hours and let the animals out. Find him online at *gideonsterer.com*.

Mariachiara Di Giorgio is an illustrator, storyboard artist and concept designer from Rome, Italy. She created the wordless picture book *Professional Crocodile*, with writer Giovanna Zoboli in 2017. Find Mariachiara online at mariachiaradigiorgio.com

Available from all good booksellers

www.walker.co.uk